THE LIFE & TIMES OF
SADDAM HUSSEIN

THE LIFE & TIMES OF

Saddam Hussein

BY
Amy Dempsey

||| •PARRAGON• |||

This edition first published by
Parragon Book Service Ltd in 1996

Parragon Book Service Ltd
Unit 13–17 Avonbridge Trading Estate
Atlantic Road, Avonmouth
Bristol BS11 9QD

Produced by Magpie Books,
an imprint of Robinson Publishing

Illustrations courtesy of: Hulton Deutsch;
Mirror Syndication International;
Peter Newark's Pictures

ISBN 0 75251 582 9

A copy of the British Library Cataloguing in Publication
Data is available from the British Library.

Typeset by Whitelaw & Palmer Ltd, Glasgow
Printed in Singapore

EARLY LIFE

Madman, Monster, Megalomaniac, 'The Butcher of Baghdad' – who is the man of the Middle East who has garnered such titles, where did he come from, and how has he remained in power for over fifteen years?

Some hundred miles north of Baghdad on the Tigris River is the town of Tikrit, the birthplace, in 1138, of the famed sultan Saladin, the legendary Muslim leader who crushed the Crusaders to liberate Jerusalem from Christian rule. Almost eight hundred years later, Tikrit was to be the birthplace of a modern Iraqi ruler who aimed to emulate his predecessor's glory. Saddam Hussein was born on 28 April 1937 in his uncle Khairallah Talfah's mud hut in Al-Auja, a village on the outskirts of Tikrit. In varying accounts, Saddam's father, Hussein al-Majid al-Tikriti, was either killed by bandits or abandoned the family. In any event, his mother, Sabha, was desperately poor and after having the baby at her brother's house left him to be brought up by Khairallah's family. They named the child Saddam, meaning 'one who confronts' or 'clasher', which time would prove to be an apt name.

In 1941 Khairallah, an ardent Arab nationalist and Nazi sympathizer, participated in the Prime Minister Rashid Ali's unsuccessful anti-

British coup, and was discharged from the Iraqi army and imprisoned for five years. In the meantime, Sabha had persuaded her late husband's younger brother, Hasan Ibrahim, to abandon his wife and marry her. The young Saddam had to leave his uncle's family and move to the small, rural village of al-Shawish to live with his mother and cruel stepfather. The family was very poor and the village had no paved roads, electricity or running water. As Saddam himself recalls, 'life was difficult everywhere in Iraq. Very few people wore shoes. And in many cases they only wore them on special occasions. Some peasants would not put their shoes on until they had reached their destination, so they would look smart.'

Saddam's early childhood experiences were harsh ones. Whereas Khairallah's family had a relatively high social standing as a result of his being a military officer, his stepfather was a village thug known locally as 'Hasan the liar'. Hasan was a sadistic brute who amused himself by torturing and humiliating the young Saddam. A common punishment was to beat Saddam with an asphalt-covered stick, forcing him to dance around to avoid the blows. When Saddam wanted to start school, his stepfather forbade him, sending him out to steal for him instead. The young Saddam had no friends in the village and was teased by the local boys for being fatherless. He carried an iron bar for protection, which, according to exiled sources, he also used to entertain himself with by heating the bar up and stabbing passing animals with it, splitting them in half. In response to such reports Saddam tells of his love for his horse, when it died Saddam was so distraught that his hand was paralysed for a week: Saddam comments, 'a relationship between man and animal, can at times be more affectionate, intimate, and unselfish than relations between two human beings.' At an early age he became tough and street-smart, for the early lessons he learned were of man's inhumanity to man, always to be on guard, to attack before being attacked, and never to trust those close to you.

Saddam greatly preferred life with his uncle, and in 1947, at the age of ten, he left his mother and stepfather and returned to Khairallah's home in Tikrit. He was enrolled at the local primary school and with the support and encouragement of his uncle managed to make it through. His cousin, Adnan, three years younger than Saddam, was also a source of support and became his best friend. In 1955 he finished primary school and followed his uncle to Baghdad where he enrolled at the al-Karkh secondary school at the age of eighteen. Wanting to be a soldier like his uncle, he applied to the Baghdad Military Academy, but failed the entrance examinations. These were turbulent times in Iraq with an upsurge in nationalist fervour, and Saddam soon found political activism much more interesting than school work. While at school he became involved with the Arab Ba'ath Socialist Party and in 1956 took part in an abortive coup attempt against the pro-British Iraqi monarchy of King Faisal II. In 1957, at the age of twenty, he formally joined the Ba'ath Party.

PARTY MEMBER

The Ba'ath Party, the party of the Resurrection, is a radical, modernizing party whose ideology is a mixture of pan-Arabism and socialism. Its primary goal is the elimination of 'traces of colonialism' and the unification of the Arab nation. Although the party was small, in 1957 its nationalist ideals were the same that Saddam had absorbed from his uncle. Saddam threw himself into party activities, including organizing anti-government student activities. He was jailed for six months in 1958 for his part in the murder of a government official in Tikrit. He was then one of ten young men chosen by the Ba'ath leadership to assassinate Prime Minister Abdul Karim Kassem, who had overthrown King Faisal II in 1958. In October 1959, they ambushed Kassem's car and shot him at close range. Wounded, but surviving, Kassem ordered a clampdown on the Ba'ath Party. This abortive assassination attempt brought both the Ba'ath Party and Saddam out of obscurity into notoriety. Saddam's official role in the assassination was to provide cover for his comrades, but his role and following escape have since been embellished and exaggerated as part of the mythology of the President. He has since been cast as the young idealistic revolutionary armed only with a pistol to take on the hated dictator. Wounded in the attempt and on the run, he unflinch-

Abdul Karin Kassem and Ahmed Hassan al-Bakr

ingly cuts the bullet out of his leg, swims the Tigris, steals a donkey and rides off to cross the desert to Syria disguised as a Bedouin tribesman. Whatever the actual events, Saddam fled to Syria and was sentenced to death in absentia for his part in the attack.

After three months in Syria, passage to Cairo was arranged for Saddam by the Egyptian President Gamal Abdel Nasser, who had heard of his part in the attempt to kill Kassem. Cairo was the centre of pan-Arabism and Saddam was quickly integrated in the community of political activists and exiles there and joined the Egyptian branch of the Ba'ath Party, becoming a member of its Regional Command. He received a stipend from the Egyptian government as an Iraqi Ba'ath in exile and returned to his education. In 1961, at the age of twenty-four, he finally graduated from secondary

President Gamel Abdel Nasser of Egypt

school and a year later began a law degree at the University of Cairo. His time in Egypt allowed him to observe the revolutionary political rhetoric of President Nasser up close. Nasser advocated an independent Arab state from 'the Atlantic to the Gulf', free from Western control and influence, and his political tactics included the dismantling of party pluralism in favour of a single-party system.

While in Cairo, Saddam decided to marry his cousin, Sajida Talfah, whom he had grown up with while living with his uncle. Following tradition, he contacted his stepfather, Hasan Ibrahim, to ask Khairallah on his behalf for his daughter's hand in marriage. Khairallah consented and the couple were engaged in 1962 while Saddam was still in exile.

In February 1963, Kassem was overthrown and

executed by the Ba'athists in Iraq and a new
government was formed under Ba'ath Party
leadership. Saddam returned to Baghdad and
married Sajida. The wedding photograph
shows a happy, relaxed, good-looking couple.
Saddam had yet to grow his characteristic
moustache and develop his tough, hard look
that would become familiar. Their first son,
Udai, was born a year later.

Upon his return to Baghdad, Saddam became
active again in the Ba'ath Party, participating in
its fourth regional and sixth national con-
gresses. His main interest was in security matters and he pushed for the formation of a special
security body to protect the Party against army
coups. The body, the Jihaz Haneen, was to be
modelled on the Nazi SS. He also enrolled at
al-Mustansiriyah University to continue his
law studies.

In November 1963, the Ba'ath regime was overthrown and Saddam went underground. He continued to work on the build up of the Jihaz Haneen, to experiment with different methods of torture, and to plot the assassination of the entire Iraqi leadership. In October 1964, he was found by the authorities and imprisoned for two years until he escaped. During his time behind bars, he continued his law studies and honed his leadership skills on his fellow prisoners. Upon his escape, he again went underground where he worked on reorganizing the Ba'ath Party and setting out its propaganda for the revolution.

In a bloodless coup in July 1968 the Ba'ath Party regained power. The head of the Party's military wing, Major-General Ahmed Hassan al-Bakr, was made President, with Saddam as

his secretary and the acting deputy of the
Revolutionary Command Council. In 1966,
Saddam was made deputy chairman of the
Council, the second most important post in
the new government. The Jihaz Haneen was
the dominant security force, with Saddam in
charge of deciding who should be issued fire-
arms. Through the Jihaz Haneen, he set about
purging those who he thought might threaten
the Party's power or his position in it. One
notable example was the hanging of fourteen
convicted 'spies', eleven of them Jewish, on
27 January 1969 in Baghdad's Liberation
Square. The Party brought around 100,000
'workers and peasants' into the city centre to
turn the event into a festival. The event lasted
twenty-four hours, with numerous anti-
Zionist and anti-imperialist speeches from
Bakr and family picnics in the square. Saddam
later commented that the men were hanged

'to teach the people a lesson' – the Ba'athists were here to stay.

Saddam continued his law studies, taking the degree by his own means. According to an account in the London *Observer*, 'In 1969 he added a law degree to his other honours by the simple expedient of turning up in the examination hall with a pistol in his belt and accompanied by four armed bodyguards. The examiners got the point.' He also felt it necessary to have military standing and in 1973 he received the rank of lieutenant-general, and in 1976 he had Bakr confer the rank of full general upon him, retroactive to 1973, making him senior to all other generals. He also obtained an honorary MS in military science in 1976.

The Bakr-Hussein regime continued to

Saddam Hussein speaking at a rally, 1970

consolidate their power and to purge any dissidents, perceived or real. Jews, Muslims, government officials, members of the Ba'athist Old Guard, and even former friends of Saddam's were amongst those executed. As Saddam's power grew, so too did his reputation for brutality. Many of the worst cases of torture took place at the infamous Qasr al-Nihayah, the 'Palace of the End'. One Shi'ite survivor tells of Saddam's hands-on role, 'He came into the room, picked up Dukhail and dropped him into a bath of acid. And then he watched while the body dissolved.' A 'revolutionary court' was established to deal with 'spies, agents, and enemies of the people', who were charged with 'conspiracy to overthrow the government' and 'espionage on behalf of the United States, Israel or Iran'. Men were forced from office, exiled, imprisoned, assassinated or executed –

some with their whole families – leading
Amnesty International to classify Iraq as one
of the worst violators of human rights. Many
of the show trials were televised to the Iraqi
people.

Even those in the Ba'athist party were not safe
if Saddam perceived them as a threat to his
eventual leadership of the party, so they were
exiled or executed. An abortive attempt by
Colonel Nazem Kazzar, head of the security
forces, to overthrow Bakr and Saddam led to
mass executions. Saddam made good his boast
that, 'with our Party methods, there is no
chance of anyone who disagrees with us to
jump on a couple of tanks and overthrow the
government'. 'Traitors' and 'spies' continued
to be executed and their families sent invoices
for the cost of the bullets used to kill them.
Throughout the 1960s and '70s, Bakr and

Saddam successfully removed any opposition to their leadership and filled positions in the security forces, military, and civilian sectors with their relatives and supporters.

Having consolidated their power, the Bakr-Hussein regime turned to economic matters. In 1972 Saddam began the nationalization of the foreign-owned Iraq Petroleum Company, which produced about ten per cent of Middle-Eastern oil. By the mid-1970s, Iraq was the second-largest oil producer in the Middle East and much of this new wealth was used on ambitious social and educational reforms, including agricultural modernization, the building of industrial plants, hospitals, housing, highways and rural electrification. A national compulsory literacy programme was launched in 1978 and higher education was stressed to create a 'new technological Arab generation'.

In 1972, Saddam travelled to Moscow to formalize relations with the Soviet Union, and in the coming years the USSR would be Iraq's primary arms supplier. Iraq had severed diplomatic relations with the United States because of its support for Israel in the 1967 Six Day War, and in 1973 the Iraqi government sent 18,000 troops to take part in the Arab war against Israel, but despite this, during the 1970s, trade with the United States increased. While still promoting nationalism and socialism as the party line, by the late 1970s almost total industrial investment was in national capitalist ventures and foreign multinationals.

Closer to home, the long-standing conflict with Iran was temporarily defused when Saddam met with the Shah of Iran in March 1975 and worked out border disputes. The

Vice President Saddam Hussein, 1975

Iraqi government compromised on the Shatt al-Arab waterway, so that the median line would be recognized as the boundary. For their part, Iran agreed to end its support of the Kurdish rebels seeking autonomy in northern Iraq. This effectively ended the ongoing civil war that had claimed 60,000 Iraqi casualties in 1974–5.

THE PRESIDENT

On National Day, 17 July 1979, Saddam
Hussein declared himself President of Iraq.
Bakr was said to have resigned due to ill
health and was placed under house arrest. As
Saddam became head of state, he also became
chairman of the Revolutionary Command
Council, Prime Minister, commander of the
armed forces, and Secretary-General of the
Ba'ath Party. Five days after taking office, he
claimed to have uncovered a Syrian-backed
plot against him and carried out a terror purge

Saddam Hussein, President of Iraq

in a closed session of the Party, theatrically reading out the names of the 'traitors', who were then led out to the firing squad. In the words of Saddam, 'We are now in our Stalinist era. We shall strike with an iron fist against the slightest deviation or backsliding, beginning with the Ba'athists themselves.'

Saddam merged several ministeries and created new posts which he filled with his Tikriti relatives. Saddam's cousin, Adnan Khairallah Talfah, his childhood friend, was made Minister of Defence and another relative, Sa'dun Shakir, was made Minister of the Interior. To keep the support of the Kurds, several Kurdish figures were appointed to senior positions in the Party. In June 1980, an election was held for the new 250-seat National Assembly. The state legislature had lain dormant since the overthrow of the monarchy in 1958. There were, however, strict qualifications for candidates, including being 'a believer in the principles of the July Revolution', which effectively ruled out any oppostion. Saddam's position was made clear to the Iraqi people on election day, 'We must ensure that the thirteen and a half million Iraqis take the same road. He who chooses the twisted path, will meet the sword.' Of the 250 members elected, only seventeen were 'independent' representatives, the rest being Ba'ath Party members. The 'election' served to give an appearance of democracy and to demonstrate that, 'Saddam Hussein is the hope of the Arab nation and the Arab homeland'.

A vigorous personality cult campaign was launched, with portraits of Saddam appearing everywhere and almost nightly television appearances. He was shown helping farmers, giving sweets to children, visiting factories, and his personal telephone number was made publicly available for citizens wishing to discuss their problems with him. His heroic past was featured in newspapers, made into a film and an exhibition in Baghdad. The young, dynamic President was the omnipresent father figure, demanding unconditional love and support, but chosen to lead his people forward. The Saddam presented to the Iraqi people was a devoted family man with two sons, Udai and Qusai, and three daughters, Raghd, Rina and Hala, a man who enjoyed gardening and fishing and tending the family sheep in his spare time.

Although the image presented to the people was that of a man of the people with simple needs and tastes, Saddam in private enjoyed the privileges of his new position. A luxury yacht was built for him by a Danish shipyard and his wardrobe is rumoured to contain over 200 expensive suits, military uniforms and tribal costumes for every occasion. An assistant follows him around with a large box of Havana cigars, which, along with the burly moustache, has become one of his trademarks.

Iraq's wealth from oil continued to grow such that by 1980 there were around 700 multimillionaires, most connected in some way to the Ba'ath Party. Office buildings, housing, and hotels sprung up and higher education and medical care were made free to the masses. Poverty was virtually eliminated and the Iraqi government gave money to poorer nations. Some gains were made for women, with legislation providing for equal pay and outlawing sex discrimination in job selection.

In 1978, amendments were introduced to the Code of Personal Status which made polygamy more difficult and gave women a greater degree of choice in marriage and divorce. Women were also allowed to enrol in the Party Militia and the military.

The oil revenue, estimated at $26 billion in 1980, also allowed Saddam to strengthen the military and state security forces. One such organization is the Mukhabarat, or the General Intelligence Department, which grew out of Saddam's secret police, the Jihaz Haneen. The Mukhabarat is responsible for monitoring the other policing organizations and controlling the activities of various state and corporate institutions. Saddam's half-brother, Barzan Ibrahim al-Tikriti, headed the Department from 1974 to 1983, to be followed by Fadel Barrak, a supporter of Bakr and Saddam, and then a cousin of Saddam's, and at the end of 1989 another half-brother, Sabawi. The State Internal Security, Amn al-Amm, is reportedly run by Saddam's youngest half-brother, Wathban, and the Soviet Union helped to develop the organ and supplied it with surveillance and interrogation equipment. The Estikhbarat, Military Intelligence, runs terrorist operations against selected targets and Iraqis living abroad. Iraqis have been assassinated in the United States, Lebanon, Sweden, Britain, Egypt, and the Sudan. Hussein Kamal al-Majid, Saddam's cousin and son-in-law, is involved in the Amn al-Khass, the Presidential Affairs Department. In addition, there is a Party Security force to survey Party members, and Border Guards, various police forces, Party Militia, the Iraqi Army, and the General Department of Nationality.

Another obsession of Saddam's was the build-
up of nuclear weapons, for they represented
to him both Iraq's arrival in the technical age
and the ultimate security measure. He
purchased the Osiraq research reactor from
France in 1976, which was to be operational
by the end of 1981. Saddam also began
recruiting Arab scientists and technicians from
all over the world to build chemical and
biological weapons. The first chemical warfare plant was completed by the time he
became President in 1979.

The Iraqi Ba'ath rely on surveillance, purges,
torture and execution and the fear that such
measures inspire. Both Amnesty International
and Middle East Watch have frequently
reported on the torture and repression in a
country where twenty-four activities are
punishable by death, including 'concealment

by Ba'ath Party members of their former political affiliations', and where freedom of expression is non-existent, most Western news media are banned and a special licence is needed to own a typewriter.

IRAN–IRAQ WAR

Age-old tensions between Iran and Iraq flared up in the second year of Saddam's reign and the temporary peace accorded by the 1975 agreement was soon shattered. The Ayatollah Ruholla Khomeini of Iran had been living in exile in Iraq since 1965, where he was closely allied with the Ayatollah Baqir al-Sadr whose aim was to establish an Islamic republic in Iraq. The Shah belatedly insisted that Iraq expel Khomeini in October 1978. The Iranian religious leader settled in Paris where he had much greater freedom to plan his revolution against the Shah than in Iraq where he was under constant surveillance. Khomeini's goal was to abolish Arab or state nationalism for the higher unity of Islam. From Paris he listed his enemies, 'First, the Shah; then the American Satan; then Saddam Hussein and his infidel Ba'ath Party.'

As soon as the Ayatollah Khomeini came to power in Iran in February 1979, he began inciting the Iraqi Shi'ites to overthrow the Ba'ath government. A terrorist campaign was organized and Saddam put the Ayatollah al-Sadr, Khomeini's ally, under house arrest. Shi'ites rioted in Baghdad and Saddam responded heavily. In April 1980 he hanged al-Sadr and his sister and expelled some 40,000 Shi'ites to Iran, arresting, torturing and executing hundreds more. Upon hearing

Ayatollah Ruholla Khomeini of Iran

of the death of al-Sadr, Khomeini declared, 'The war that the Iraqi Ba'ath wants to ignite is a war against Islam . . . The people and army of Iraq must turn their backs on the Ba'ath regime and overthrow it . . .'.

The Khomeini regime had also alienated the United States and the Soviet Union and Saddam did not want their intervention in the matter as it might threaten his plans for hegemony over the Persian Gulf region. Iran's lack of support made it seem an easy target. On 17 September 1980, in a televised speech to the National Assembly, Saddam claimed full control of the Shatt al-Arab waterway, negating the 1975 treaty. Five days later Saddam's armies mounted a general offensive. As the war with Iran was basically a result of animosity between Saddam and the Ayatollah, it was necessary for Saddam to convince the Iraqi people that the cause was theirs. The propaganda of the personality cult was stepped up to the extent that a popular joke was that Iraq's population had reached 28 million – 14 million Iraqis and 14 million portraits of Saddam Hussein. He was portrayed as 'father of the nation and its glorious son, a fierce warrior and a thoughtful philosopher, a radical revolutionary and a practising Muslim'. He aligned himself with historical figures such as the Prophet Muhammad and the Babylonian king Nebuchadnezzar, claiming that he was the logical descendant of the great leaders of the past and the man to promote and protect Iraqi patriotism and Arab nationalism. As he said himself: '. . . what is most important for me about Nebuchadnezzar is the link between the Arabs' ability and the liberation of Palestine. Nebuchadnezzar was, after all, an Arab from Iraq, albeit ancient Iraq. Nebuchadnezzar was the one who brought the

The Iran–Iraq war

bound Jewish slaves from Palestine. That is why whenever I remember Nebuchadnezzar I like to remind the Arabs, Iraqis in particular, of their historical responsibilities.'

Another tactic of Saddam's was to shield the general populace from the effects of the war. He wanted to prove that he could wage a war while conducting business-as-usual, and continued with development plans. The majority of the state budget was not spent on the war effort but on civilian imports to prevent any shortages. This policy shielded the Iraqis from the hardships of war and those directly affected by a death were granted a free car, a free plot of land and an interest-free loan to build a house.

After some initial territorial gains, poor leadership in the Iraqi armies and a stronger

than anticipated Iranian army, led to stale-
mate. During this, in June 1981, Israel
launched an air-strike against Iraq, destroying
the nearly operational French-built nuclear
reactor. Although Saddam claimed it was
built for peaceful purposes, the Israelis
claimed it posed a threat of nuclear attack.
The United Nations Security Council con-
demned Israel for the attack and Saddam
declared that he would 'leave for the future'
any decision about retaliation.

In 1982 Saddam reshuffled the major power
posts at the Ninth Regional Congress of the
Ba'ath Party. Unlike early changes in offices,
only one of the ousted officers was executed.
As the story goes, the Minister of Health,
Riyadh Ibrahim Hussein, suggested that
Saddam step down temporarily to make way
for a ceasefire. The President invited the

Saddam Hussein depicted as a military leader

Minister into another room to discuss the matter further, a shot was fired, and Saddam returned alone. Whether or not Saddam did personally execute the Minister, the incident served to strengthen his image as the 'strong man of Baghdad' with his mastery of the gun. Another story has him addressing the National Assembly in 1982, when he noticed one man passing a note to another and without pause drew his gun and shot the both of them. His suspicion that the note was about the time to kill the President was proved correct. In 1982 and 1983 over 300 high-ranking officers were killed by firing squad. The official reason given was 'failing their duties'. They had to pay the price for the military failures.

Saddam continued repression of the Shi'ites in Iraq, alternating with goodwill gestures. He promised that 40 per cent of those elected for the National Assembly in 1980 and 1984 would be Shi'ites, as would the Speaker. The standard of living of Shi'ites was improved and their shrines renovated. The Kurds did not fare so well. Realizing that Saddam had no intention of supporting Kurdish autonomy, in 1985 there was a full-scale insurrection in Kurdistan. A ferocious campaign was launched against them, beginning with the execution of 8,000 'prisoners' captured in 1983. Villages and towns were destroyed and half a million Kurds were placed in settlements or concentration camps.

A number of Arab states supported Iraq's efforts, fearful of Iranian fundamentalism. Jordan, Kuwait, the Sudan, and Egypt were among those who aided the Iraqi effort. Both the US and the USSR also provided support.

The 'tanker war' began in 1984 and as it escalated, Britain, France, the Netherlands, Italy and Belgium also sent warships. Saddam's main reason for instigating the 'tanker war' was to internationalize the conflict, and in this respect he succeeded.

From 1984 onwards, UN investigators reported the Iraqi deployment of chemical weapons against Iran in violation of the 1925 Geneva Protocol. Saddam's paternal cousin, Ali Hasan al-Majid was in charge of the gas attacks against the Kurds, using mustard gas, cyanide and Tabun nerve agent on unprotected civilians. The worst attack was in March 1988 on the Kurdish town of Halabja, in which 5,000 civilians were massacred and 10,000 injured.

Meanwhile, support for the war within Iran

was declining with anti-war and anti-government demonstrations escalating. Morale was particularly low after 1987 and the number of army volunteers dropped sharply. Saddam took advantage of the situation and in February 1988 launched his most ferocious offensive yet, bombing Iran's major population centres. A string of military successes followed in which territory lost to Iran earlier in the war was regained. On 18 July 1988, Iran accepted Security Council Resolution 598 on a ceasefire in the Iran–Iraq war. Saddam was able to claim victory for the war he had started eight years earlier. He had proven himself a force to be reckoned with, one who was not afraid to do whatever necessary to remain in power; be it domestic, military or civilian purges or unconventional warfare.

INTERNAL AFFAIRS

The internal affairs of Iraq are run by one
man – Saddam Hussein. The Ba'ath Party is
in charge of all state machinery and surveillance and the Party is subordinate to Saddam.
Saddam is responsible for all decision-
making, with a small number of Party faith-
ful to enforce his wishes. The only consistent
central ideology for political decisions is
Saddam's political survival, and the continuing support for his absolute leadership is
assured through education, terror, and sys-

tematic purges of dissenters, be they real or potential.

From kindergarten on, children are taught Ba'ath terminology and the xenophobic, anti-imperialist beliefs of their President. They are institutionalized into the Party ways – taught to trust no one, to inform on anyone suspected of anti-Party behaviour, including their parents. As Saddam has said, 'You must encircle the adults through their sons in addition to other means and instruments. Teach students and pupils to contradict their parents if they hear them discussing state secrets . . . You must place in every corner a son of the revolution, with a trustworthy eye and a firm mind who receives his instruction from the responsible centre of the revolution.'

Party membership is essential for a public

career and also often a requirement for acceptance to higher education. Scholarships for foreign study are only given to Party members and the National Union of Iraqi Students is responsible for monitoring students abroad, with the penalty for dissident behaviour of up to fifteen years' imprisonment with hard labour. Advancement in the Party itself is difficult. While open to all at entry level, full membership is only for the chosen few, who have proved themselves after five to ten years of absolute dedication and commitment. The Party has all members under surveillance with an extensive network of informers to report any 'suspicious' activities: the remark often made that Iraq is a nation of informers cannot be seen to be far from the truth, as family members, neighbours, co-workers and friends are all encouraged to keep an eye on each other. A state decree of November 1986 prescribes the death penalty for public insults about the President, the RCC, the Ba'ath Party or the National Assembly. One story tells of Saddam visiting a school and asking a six-year-old boy if he knew who he was. When the boy replied, 'Yes, you are the man who makes my father spit on the television every time you appear,' the boy's entire family disappeared and their house burned down. Punishment for not informing can be just as severe. The *Index on Censorship* reports the instance in August 1987 of a Party member not reporting jokes made about Saddam, which resulted in the arrest, torture and execution of him, his three sons, and his son-in-law and the family house being razed to the ground.

It is through the extensive security system that Saddam has developed since the 1960s that he

is able to exert such control. The various
branches outlined above all operate inde-
pendently of each other, all spy on each other,
and all report to Saddam himself. To ensure
loyalty, each of the departments is run by a
fellow Tikriti or relative. Nepotism is a
guiding principle of Saddam's regime. His
administration is made up of members of his
mother's family, the Talfahs, his father's
family, the Majids, and his stepfather's family,
the Ibrahims. To disguise the extent of Tikriti
involvement in power, in the late 1970s
Saddam decreed that family names denoting
one's place of birth be abolished. New ID
cards were issued and new birth certificates
were to contain only the child's first name
and father's name. For example, instead of
Saddam Hussein al-Tikriti, he was now
simply Saddam Hussein. For Saddam this was
also useful in his aim to portray himself as a

son of the whole of Iraq, not merely a region.

Saddam's children have also been used to create and strengthen the dynastic ties. His oldest son, Udai, is married to the daughter of Izzat Ibrahim, Deputy Chairman of the RCC. His younger son, Qusai, was married to the daughter of General Maher Abd al-Rashid. This marriage was supposedly dissolved after the General fell from favour after his victories in the Iran–Iraq war and Saddam perceived him as a threat. Raghd, Saddam's eldest daughter, is married to General Hussein Kamil Hasan al-Majid, her father's cousin, who is the Minister of Industry and Military Production. Hussein Kamil's brother, Saddam Kamil, is a colonel in the long-range missile unit and is married to Raghd's sister, Rina.

While being a member of Saddam's favoured

Udai standing by a poster of his father

circle brings incredible economic gains and corruption is rife, falling from favour has disastrous consequences. Saddam's uncle, Khairallah Talfah, the man who raised him, became Mayor of Baghdad shortly after Saddam came to power. He amassed an incredible fortune in real estate deals by taking advantage of his connections and forcing landowners to sell him property at ridiculously low prices. His greed and corruption reached such outrageous levels that Saddam was forced to remove him from office, and in 1990 to close seventeen companies run by Khairallah and arrest their executives. Saddam's cousin, Adnan Khairallah Talfah, who was more like a brother to him, did not fare so well. Saddam took him to the top with him, appointing him Deputy Prime Minister and Deputy Commander-in-Chief of the Armed Forces, where he served as Saddam's right-hand man during the war with

Iran. His reward included wealth that enabled him to own more than 500 cars at his death. However, even he was not safe from Saddam. His glory as a war hero and his involvement in a family affair where he sided with his sister, Saddam's wife, could not be overlooked. In May 1989 he died in a 'mysterious' helicopter crash. Other war heroes, who also made the mistake of sharing in Saddam's glory, have disappeared, believed to be under house arrest or executed.

To be in Saddam's inner circle, one must be unconditionally loyal, not too popular, and not cause embarrassment to Saddam or to his carefully constructed public image. Udai, Saddam's eldest son, has provided his share of family traumas. Upon graduating from college in 1984, he was made President of Saddam University and the Head of Iraq's Olympic

Committee. He has used his position as the President's son for incredible financial gain, acquiring a vast network of businesses and a collection of cars only slightly smaller than his uncle's. He reportedly made over $20 million in a single transaction in 1988 which involved forcing the central bank to sell him foreign currency at the official rate, which he then sold on the black market. He abused his position in personal matters as well, killing, on separate occasions, two army officers who interfered when he tried to seduce the daughter of one and the wife of the other. While these examples of corruption and murder were tolerated, Udai went too far in the 'Shahbandar Affair'.

While Saddam had always had a string of affairs, they were kept quiet, unlike his liaison with Samira Shahbandar in 1988, which became public knowledge. A family feud erupted in which Adnan Khairallah sided with his sister against the President to his later detriment, as did Udai. The scandal that followed rocked Saddam's marriage and his image as a devoted family man. The Presidential food taster had introduced Saddam to his mistress and in addition to his official capacities, served as messenger for the lovers. Udai publicly clubbed the man to death to avenge his mother's honour, and the enraged Saddam imprisoned Udai and threatened to bring murder charges against him. Only the intervention of his mother and uncle saved him, and he was instead sent into exile in Switzerland. As Sajida said to her husband, 'Why arrest him? After all, it is not the first time he has killed. Nor is he the only one in his family who has killed.' After a cooling off period, Udai was allowed to return to Baghdad in the spring of 1990 and take up where he had left off.

BETWEEN THE WARS

With the end of war with Iran in the summer of 1988, which Saddam claimed as a victory for Iraq and the Arab nation, the challenges facing Saddam were many. The removal of Iran as the common enemy that united Iraqis in support of Saddam, the existence of a huge, now unemployed army and a debt-ridden economy all threatened his political survival. The cult of personality went into overdrive with a massive triumphal arch constructed in central Baghdad of two pairs of crossed swords held by bronze fists – the fists of Saddam Hussein. Moments of glorious Iraqi history were resuscitated, including a reconstruction of Babylon, complete with inscriptions proclaiming that 'the Babylon of Nebuchadnezzar was rebuilt in the era of the leader President Saddam Hussein'. Even the Hashemite monarchy was rehabilitated as 'a symbol of Iraqi unity and continuity', all leading to Saddam as the logical successor to take Iraq into the next era.

Against all his previous political rhetoric, it was to the private sector that he turned for economic reconstruction. Many state-owned corporations were privatised, price controls were lifted, and foreign, mainly Western companies were courted for investment, with $2 billion worth of import licences granted. The plight of the Kurds came to increased international attention in 1989 but Saddam was relieved to discover that business concerns outweighed moral ones, as foreign sanctions were rejected and investment continued.

In late 1988 Saddam began 'what seemed an Iraqi perestroika'. Whether to show the Iraqi people that he did embody a new era, or to flush out political dissidents, or to combat negative press on human rights, Saddam announced a general pardon to political dissidents at home and abroad, promised a new constitution, and a democratic multi-party system, while the Information Minister commented that a free press was now of 'paramount interest'. The Iraqis elected a new National Assembly in April 1989 and Western press was flown in to witness the 'democratic' election. The Arab press was also recruited to Saddam's vision. Leading Egyptian editors reported receiving new Mercedes Benz and less influential members of the press received Toyotas.

Iraq's foreign debt at the end of the war was $80 billion, privatization was not helping the domestic economy, instead provoking a backlash of high inflation which meant that price controls had to be re-established. Two million migrant workers were forced out of Iraq to make room for returning soldiers in the work place. Women also bore the brunt of Saddam's continuing bids for support from various parts of the public. In order to gain the support of the Muslims he plunged family law back to the days of medieval Islam when, in February 1990, the RCC decreed that 'any Iraqi who, on grounds of adultery, purposely kills his mother, daughter, sister, maternal or paternal aunt, maternal or paternal niece, maternal or paternal female cousin, shall not be prosecuted.'

From 1988 to 1990 Saddam's paranoia increased as there were a number of unsuccessful attempts on his life. The coup attempt that worried him the most was staged by officers from the Republican Guard, his personal bodyguard force. As expected, it was suppressed, with hundreds of executions, but it signalled the growing unrest and dissatisfaction amongst even those closest to him. In January 1990 another attempt on his life was made by a group of army officers. These domestic incidents, combined with the fall of communist regimes in Eastern Europe, who had been the Arabs' natural allies, made the Iraqi leader very nervous. The fall of the Romanian dictator, Nicolae Ceauşescu, whose power had been consolidated through a reign of terror and the cult of personality, much like Saddam's, was a particularly worrisome event. As his fear of losing power grew, he felt it necessary to remind potential plotters that he was as strict as ever with 'traitors'. In September 1989, an Iranian-born journalist working for the London *Observer*, Farzad Bazoft, was arrested. In March 1990 he was tried on charges of espionage and executed. Whereas Saddam had been executing 'spies' and 'traitors' for years, they were always Iraqi internal affairs, but Bazoft's British affiliation provoked international outrage. The West saw this as confirmation of the brutality and unpredictability of Saddam's rule and began to take action against his build-up of non-conventional weapons. Saddam interpreted this as a smear campaign against Iraq and as further evidence of an Israeli–US conspiracy to disable Iraq.

54

To add to Saddam's growing domestic and international problems was his frustration with his Arab neighbours. Any economic solution was increasingly necessary as the Iraqi people expected not privation but the promised fruits of the 'historic victory'. During the war he had pressured Saudi Arabia and Kuwait to write off their loans to Iraq, arguing that Iraq was fighting on their behalf as well against the fundamentalist Islam of Khomeini: they too were the beneficiaries of Iraq's struggle. Saddam increased the pressure in February 1990 at the summit meeting of the Arab Cooperation Council, in which he asked King Hussein of Jordan and President Mubarak of Egypt to tell the Gulf states that not only did Iraq expect a suspension of payment on its wartime loans, but that it also needed a loan of around $30 billion. Saddam added, 'Let the Gulf regimes know that if they did not give this money to me, I would know how to get it.' This threat was backed up by Iraqi military manoeuvres on the Kuwaiti border.

Saddam's other strategy to increase revenue was to demand that other members of the Organization of Petroleum Exporting Countries (OPEC) decrease their quotas, in order that Iraq increase its production without pushing prices down. This request was completely ignored and to add insult to injury, Kuwait and the United Arab Emirates (UAE) exceeded their existing quotas, thereby driving world oil prices down. Even when Saddam referred to the continuing quota violations as a 'kind of war against Iraq', Kuwait and the UAE did not bend. The Emir of Kuwait steadfastly refused to forgive Iraq's war debts, decrease oil production, or give

Iraq further funds. To make matters worse, Kuwait had been drilling oil, to a value of $2.4 billion, from a field that crosses the Kuwait/Iraq border. Only in July 1990 at a meeting of Gulf oil ministers did the UAE and Kuwait finally concede to the combined pressures of the Saudis, Iranians, and Iraqis and agreed to abide by their oil quotas.

THE INVASION
OF KUWAIT

It was too little too late. Saddam continued to
accuse Kuwait and the UAE of conspiring
with 'world imperialism and Zionism' and
demanded that the two states come 'back to
their senses'. He presented them with the
ultimatum that 'if words fail to afford us
protection, then we will have no choice but
to resort to effective action to put things right
and ensure the restitution of our rights'. The
Kuwaitis did not take his demands seriously

and negotiations fell apart on 1 August. On Thursday, 2 August 1990 Iraq invaded Kuwait. 100,000 Iraqi troops and 300 tanks effectively crushed any opposition and occupied the country. It was presented to the Iraqi people as a short-term measure and that forces would be withdrawn 'as soon as the situation settles down and the evil grip is loosened on Arab Kuwait'.

International indignation and response was swift. President George Bush placed an economic embargo against Iraq almost immediately, and all Kuwaiti and Iraqi assets and property in American banks and companies were frozen. The United States and the Soviet Union issued a condemnation of the invasion, as did the UN Security Council. The European Community and Japan followed suit by imposing economic sanctions and the

Soviet Union and China discontinued all arms shipments. The UN Security Council passed Resolution 661, ordering worldwide economic sanctions and an arms embargo on Iraq, and Turkey closed down the Iraqi oil pipeline that passed through it. Within a few days, Saddam's conflict with Kuwait had become Iraq against almost the whole of the international community.

On 8 August, President Bush made a televised address to the American public announcing his decision to send troops to Saudi Arabia at their request. Bush's policy called for the immediate, unconditional and complete Iraqi withdrawal from Kuwait; the restoration of the legitimate Kuwait government; the assurance of Gulf security and stability; and the protection of the lives of American citizens abroad. He labelled

Hussein an 'aggressive dictator threatening his neighbours'. Saddam was now backed into a corner, for any withdrawal would be seen as bowing to the 'infidel' Western power, and his pride could allow no such thing. He responded by announcing the merger of Iraq and Kuwait, and on 28 August Kuwait became the nineteenth province of Iraq.

Saddam announced his peace proposal on 12 August in which he linked the issue of Kuwait with the problem of Palestine. His solution called for 'the immediate and unconditional withdrawal of Israel from the occupied Arab territories in Palestine, Syria, and Lebanon, Syria's withdrawal from Lebanon, and a withdrawal between Iraq and Iran.' After these conditions were met a solution for Kuwait could arise, 'taking into consideration the historical rights of Iraq to its land and the choice of the

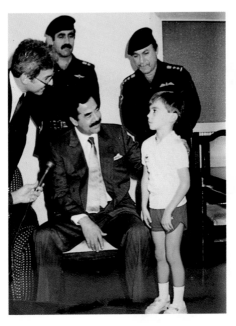

Saddam Hussein talking to young hostage,
Stewart Lockwood, 1990

Kuwaiti people'. While his proposal was rejected, it did inject the Arab–Israeli issue into future peace initiatives for the Gulf crisis.

Saddam's wartime strategies against the West took the form of divide and conquer. He tried to break up the unity of the coalition through anti-American propaganda, cash incentives, and hostage bargaining. He allowed the release of a number of hostages and promised the release of many more in order to try to stall the inevitable UN resolution authorizing the use of force to liberate Kuwait. This tactic did not work and on 29 November the UN Security Council passed Resolution 678, which called for Iraq to leave Kuwait by mid-January or military force would be deployed to enforce it. A last-ditch effort for negotiations between the US and Iraq was suggested, but neither Saddam or Bush would accept the

Tariq Aziz

dates offered by the other. As another stalling attempt Saddam released all remaining hostages on 6 December. When Saddam realized that this goodwill gesture would not affect the terms of the Resolution, he began preparing for war.

The Geneva meeting between US Secretary of State, James Baker and the Iraqi Foreign Minister, Tariq Aziz, was a failure, as Baker's announcement made clear: 'Saddam Hussein continues to reject a diplomatic solution.' The Revolutionary Command Council issued an announcement stating that, 'the belief that Kuwait is part of Iraq is unshakeable, and that it is the nineteenth province is a fact treated by our people and their Armed Forces as a great gain . . . It has become a symbol of honour and virtue in this major battle – the mother of battles.'

THE MOTHER OF
ALL BATTLES

On Thursday, 17 January 1991 war began. Military, strategic and political targets were hit in the first wave. Iraqi state radio announced: 'The great duel, the mother of all battles, between victorious right and the evil that will certainly be defeated has begun, God willing.' Saddam portrayed the conflict as a holy war between Islam and the evil infidels. His main strategy was to try to push the West into a premature ground battle in Kuwait that

The Gulf war: patriot missiles fired into Saudi Arabia from Iraq

would bring the war to a quick end. With this aim in mind he sent ballistic missiles into Israel. Israeli restraint was not what he had bargained for, neither was the condemnation of his actions by his fellow Arabs. Saddam's next tactic was to inflict ecological disaster by setting light to several oil installations in Kuwait and pumping oil into the Persian Gulf. He again employed hostages as 'human shields' and televised captured allied airmen. These ploys also backfired, leading to further commitment to the liberation of Kuwait and the warning that Saddam would be tried for war crimes after the war.

As fighting continued, civilian life in Baghdad deteriorated dramatically. There was no electricity or running water and an indefinite halt on the sale of fuel was announced in February. Saddam began to consider a peace initiative proposed by Moscow. His delaying tactics did him no favours, as Bush announced that he had until 28 February to begin withdrawing troops. Saddam publicly rejected this ultimatum and within forty-eight hours of the land offensive the Iraqi army had been broken, with Iraqi forces surrendering by the thousands. On 26 February, Saddam announced the withdrawal of forces from Kuwait.

Saddam presented the withdrawal not as a defeat, but as a victory to his people, 'Applaud your victories, my dear citizens. You have faced thirty countries and the evil they have brought here. You have faced the whole world, great Iraqis. You have won. You are victorious. How sweet victory is.' Iraq eventually agreed to comply with the Security Council resolutions and on 28 February, six

Iraqi prisoners held by allied troops, 1991

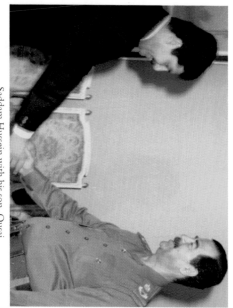

Saddam Hussein with his son, Qusai

weeks after the launching of Desert Storm, the coalition fighting was suspended, pending a permanent ceasefire.

Saddam again presented to his people the 'glorious Iraqi victory'. For Saddam though, it was on to the next challenge in his battle for personal and political survival. When he came to power in 1979 Iraq was a regional economic superpower, with billions of barrels of oil and the most powerful army in the Arab world. After two wars in twelve years, the country is impoverished, its army destroyed, and it has a foreign debt of over $80 billion. His legacy includes hundreds of thousands of Iraqi casualties and economic and ecological disaster. In his quest for personal survival he has sacrificed everything and everyone around him and it is the people of Iraq who continue to pay the price.

Since the end of the Gulf War, Saddam's problems have escalated. UN economic sanctions imposed in 1990 still stand, crippling the country's economy. The Iraqi dinar has been so devalued that an average salary in Baghdad is now around $2 a month. In the twenty-six years of Saddam's rule, Iraq has gone from being one of the world's wealthiest systems, to a nation on the verge of starvation. He blames these problems on the West, particularly Britain and the US, who are the primary supporters of the UN sanctions.

As conditions worsen in Iraq, many Iraqis are fleeing the country. There are over 30,000 Iraqis seeking asylum in Jordan – the most famous being members of Saddam's family itself. General Hussein Kamil Hassan al-Majid, once Saddam's right-hand man, and his brother Saddam Kamil, both married to

Hussein Kamel Hussan, Saddam's son-in-law who defected to Jordan

Saddam Hussein after his re-election as President, 1995

Saddam's daughters, defected to Jordan with their families in August 1995. This defection was prompted by the increasingly sadistic and tyrannical behaviour of Saddam's eldest son, Udai. The week prior to Hussein Kamil's defection, Udai killed his half-uncle, Wathbam Ibrahim. Udai and Qusai, Saddam's two sons, are the only remaining family members on whom Saddam can rely, for there is no one left to purge. In February 1996, having been granted a pardon by Saddam, the sons-in-law returned to Iraq with their families and were brutally murdered less than a week later.

Throughout it all, Saddam Hussein remains adamant that he is the victor and that the West is the enemy to be overcome. Five years after the conflict, many of his enemies' political and military leaders at the time of the Gulf War are retired, out of office or dead! While his people can still be united by anti-American rhetoric and controlled by fear, their desperation and the crumbling of the Tikriti infrastructure that guaranteed his political survival, may be what finally bring him down, rather than some outside force.

FURTHER MINI SERIES
INCLUDE

ILLUSTRATED POETS

Robert Burns
Shakespeare
Oscar Wilde
Emily Dickinson
Christina Rossetti
Shakespeare's Love Sonnets

FURTHER MINI SERIES INCLUDE

HEROES OF THE WILD WEST

General Custer
Butch Cassidy and the Sundance Kid
Billy the Kid
Annie Oakley
Buffalo Bill
Geronimo
Wyatt Earp
Doc Holliday
Sitting Bull
Jesse James